OTHER HELEN EXLEY GIFTBOOKS IN THIS SERIES:
Over 30's Jokes
A Triumph of Over 50's Jokes
Over 70's Jokes
A Round of Golf Jokes
A Spread of Over 40's Jokes
A Jubilee of Over 60's Jokes
Old Wrecks' Jokes
A Romp of Naughty Jokes

Published in 1998 by Helen Exley Giftbooks in Great Britain.
Selection and arrangement copyright © Helen Exley 1998
Cartoons copyright © Bill Stott 1998
The moral rights of the authors have been asserted.

12 11 10 9 8 7 6 5 4 3 2

Cartoons by Bill Stott.
Edited by Claire Lipscomb.
Series Editor: Helen Exley.

ISBN: 978-1-84634-229-5

A copy of the CIP data is available from the British Library on request. All rights reserved. No part of this publication may be reproduced or transmitted in any form or by any means, electronic or mechanical, including photocopy, recording or any information storage and retrieval system without permission in writing from the publisher.
Printed in China.

Acknowledgements: A very special thank you to the following individuals who have contributed so much to this book: Sarah Woods, Richard Mason, Lynne Clark, Jane Cox, Chloe Mills, Valerie MacDonald, Dave Cole, Peter Cox, Chris Wright, Dawn Cole, Thomas Hardy, Chris Hutter, Ronald Tse, Daniel Hardy.

Helen Exley Giftbooks, 16 Chalk Hill, Watford, Herts WD19 4BG, UK.
www.helenexleygiftbooks.com

A CHUCKLE OF KIDS JOKES

CARTOONS BY
BILL STOTT

HELEN EXLEY

CRAZY CREEPIES

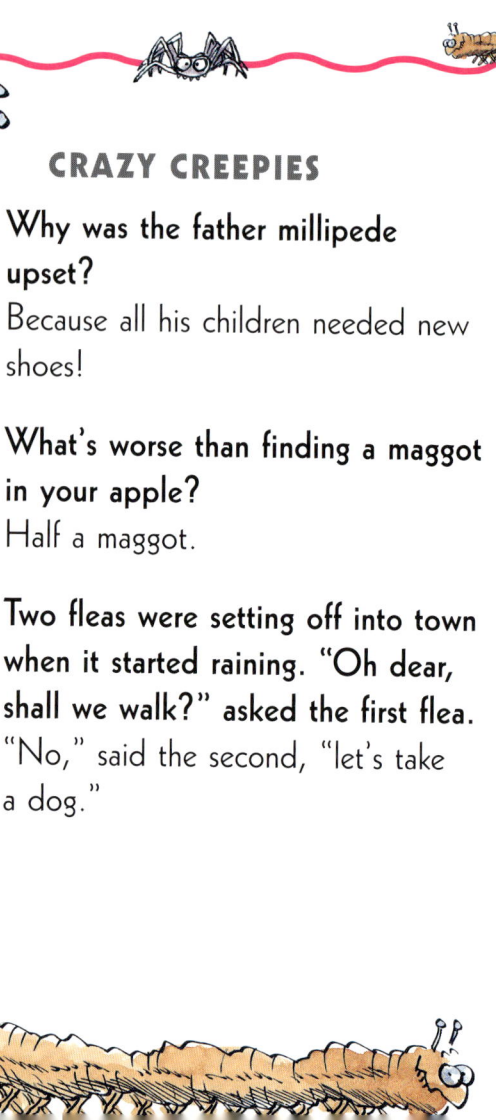

Why was the father millipede upset?
Because all his children needed new shoes!

What's worse than finding a maggot in your apple?
Half a maggot.

Two fleas were setting off into town when it started raining. "Oh dear, shall we walk?" asked the first flea. "No," said the second, "let's take a dog."

How do you tell a worm's head from his tail?
Tickle it in the middle and see which end smiles!

What's yellow and scaly, with 100 slimy tentacles and evil-looking eyes?
   I don't know.
I don't know either, but there's one on your head!

Why did the girl snail break up with the boy slug?
She said he was moving too fast.

Maria: Dad, would you punish me for something I hadn't done?
Dad: Of course not, Maria!
Maria: Good, because I haven't done the dishes.

Teenager: Dad, do you believe in free speech?
Dad: Of course, Kelvin.
Teenager: Great — I'll use the telephone then.

The mother had put her little boy to bed, and thought he had fallen asleep, when he came downstairs and asked, "Can I have a glass of water?" The mother gave him a glass, and off he went to bed. However, a few minutes later he was back, asking for more water. The mother wondered how he could be so thirsty, but gave the water to him anyway. A minute later the kid was back, "Can I have another glass of water?" he asked. "What's wrong with you!" exclaimed his mother. "That's the third glass of water tonight. How come you're so thirsty?"

"Oh!" said the little boy. "The water's not for me. The roof's on fire."

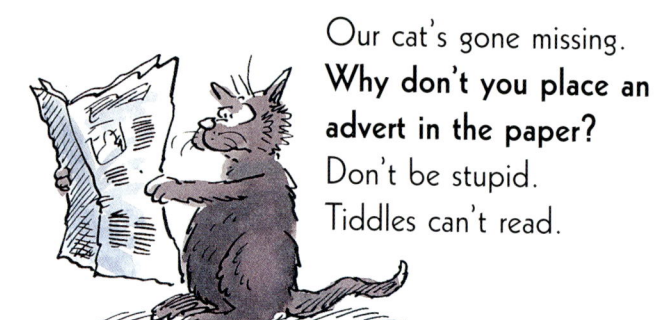

Our cat's gone missing. **Why don't you place an advert in the paper?** Don't be stupid. Tiddles can't read.

First sheep: Baa-baa.
Second sheep: Moo-ooo-ooo.
First sheep: What do you mean "Moo-ooo-ooo"?
Second sheep: I'm learning a foreign language.

Why do animals have fur coats?
Because they'd look stupid in raincoats!

A penguin walked into a cafe and ordered a cheese and lettuce sandwich. The waitress served the sandwich, and the penguin sat down at a corner table, got out his paper, and quietly ate his lunch.
Another customer, who'd observed all this with amazement, exclaimed to the waitress, "Well, I've never seen anything like it!"
"Yes," said the waitress, "most customers have tomato in their cheese sandwiches."

MONSTROUS!!

Why did the monster have bad breath?
Well, it takes a long time to clean a thousand teeth.

HOW DO YOU INTRODUCE YOURSELF TO AN ALIEN WITH THREE HEADS?

DON'T KNOW

HELLO, HELLO, HELLO!

Baby Monster: I hate Dad's guts…
Ma Monster: Well, just eat your pudding then.

Frankenstein Monster: Doctor, I've got a sore hand.
Doctor: Well, that's not too serious...
Frankenstein Monster: Yes, but this one's sewn on my head.

What did the Moon Monster say when it saw the rocket landing?

Yum. Canned people.

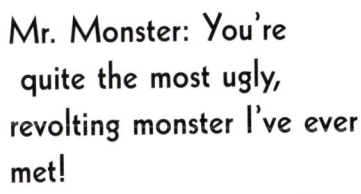

Mr. Monster: You're quite the most ugly, revolting monster I've ever met!

Mrs. Monster: Why thank you, you're not so attractive yourself.

GRUMPS AND GROUSERS

The lady next door is so rude. One day our dad was walking the dog past her house, when she shouted out of the window, "What are you doing with that smelly beast?"
Dad angrily replied, "Rover's not smelly at all!"
"Shut up!" she bellowed. "I was talking to the dog not you."

Excuse me, Sir, what time is it?
Time you got a new watch.

Woman: Did you save my dog from drowning?
Man: Yes, I did.
Woman: Well, where's his collar?

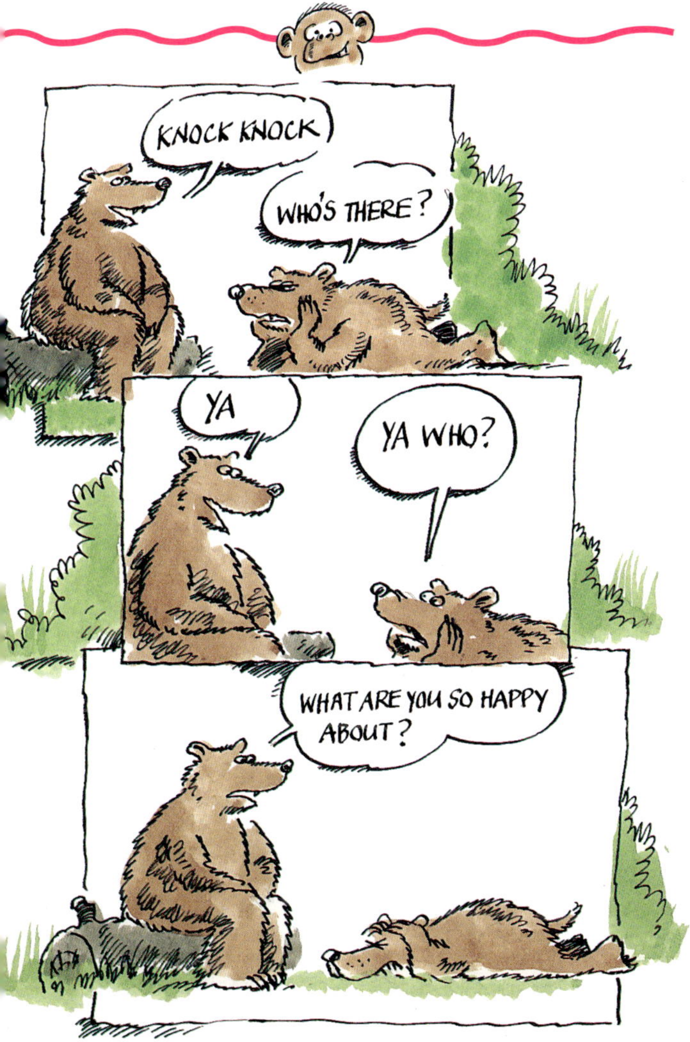
KNOCK KNOCK
WHO'S THERE?
YA
YA WHO?
WHAT ARE YOU SO HAPPY ABOUT?

WITH THE CHEF'S COMPLIMENTS

Waiter, waiter there's a dead beetle in my salad!
Yes, it's the salad dressing that kills them, Sir…

Customer: Waitress, I'd like some rotten potatoes and underdone steak, with some lumpy gravy please.
Waitress: I'm sorry, Madam, but I couldn't serve you such a meal.
Customer: Why not? You did yesterday.

Waiter, you've got your thumb on my steak!
Yes, Madam, it's to stop it falling on the floor again.

Waiter, waiter, is this tea or coffee? It tastes of mud.
It's our coffee, Sir, the tea tastes of dishwater.

Waiter, waiter, there's a fly in my soup!
Don't worry Madam, the spider in
the butter will get it.

Inventor: I've got a problem with my new super-computer.
Professor: What, the most compact computer in the world ever? What's the problem?
Inventor: It's so small I can't find the on-switch!

Why won't cyberpets ever replace real dogs?
Because you can't blame a cyberpet for eating your homework.

Why will computers never take the place of newspapers?
Have you ever tried making an airplane out of a computer?

A man was walking down the street when he bumped into his friend who was carrying two suitcases. "Hello," said the friend, "have I told you about my new watch. It's great. It can tell the time in every country, it's got a built-in calculator and diary, and I can log into the Internet from it...."

"Wow. That sounds great," said the first man. "So what are the suitcases for? Are you off on vacation?"

"No," said his friend, "these are the batteries for my watch."

What do you call a bad-tempered gorilla?
Sir.

What do you get if you cross a tiger with a flower?
I don't know.
I don't know either but I wouldn't want to smell it.

How can you tell if a horse has been in your fridge?
Hoof marks in your butter.

How can you tell if there's an elephant under your armchair?
The ceiling looks very close.

What's worse than a shark with toothache?
A giraffe with a sore throat.

CLASSROOM CAPERS

What's the difference between a boring teacher and a boring book?
You can shut up the book.

Teacher: Kirsten, if I had five apples in one hand, and six apples in the other, what would I have?
Kirsten: Very big hands, Miss McIntosh.

Teacher to pupil: If I've told you once, I've told you a million times, don't exaggerate!

Teacher Monster: Child, you're the most well-behaved monster I've ever come across in all my years of teaching.
Pupil Monster: Sorry, it won't happen again.

What's the difference between school dinners and a trough of pigswill?
School dinners are served on a plate, not in a trough!

Oh Mother! Don't make me go to school today, I hate it!
You've got to, Son. For one thing you're forty-three, and for another you're the principal!

I'm afraid you are very ill...

Nonsense. I demand a second opinion.

... and you're ugly.

Doctor: Breathe out please.
Patient: Oh, are you checking my lungs?
Doctor: No, just cleaning my glasses.

A short-sighted woman went to see her doctor, who told her to eat nothing but carrots for a month. At the end of the month he guaranteed that her sight would be so good, she'd be able to see in the dark. At the end of the month the woman walked into the surgery with a long face.
"What's the matter?" asked the doctor.
"It's this diet," said the woman. "Last night, I went to put the cat out the back door, and I tripped over in the dark."
"Well, couldn't you see properly?"
"Oh I could see all right. But I tripped over my ears!"

What should you put into a chocolate bar?
Your teeth.

A strict aunt came to tea and said to her niece, "Eat up your spinach, child, and you'll grow up to be beautiful."
"Didn't they have spinach in your day Auntie?" came the reply.

What's yellow and white and speeds at 100mph?
A train-driver's cheese sandwich.

Carrots are good for your eyes.
How do you know?
Have you ever seen a rabbit wearing spectacles?

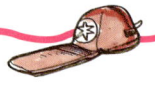

BRAIN SCRAMBLERS

What can you hold without using your hands?
Your breath.

When do 2 and 2 make five?
When you're bad at sums.

What's Winnie the Pooh's middle name?
The.

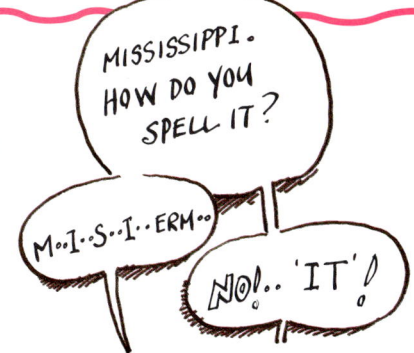

MISSISSIPPI. HOW DO YOU SPELL IT?

M..I..S..I..ERM..

NO!.. 'IT'!

Ten people were all sheltering under one small umbrella, but no one got wet. Why?
Because it wasn't raining.

Which word is always pronounced incorrectly?
Incorrectly.

What could you put into a barrel of water to make it lighter?
A hole.

What time is it when a whale sits on your sofa?
Time to get a new sofa.

Barty Bear: Why was the hyena expelled from jungle school?
Brad: I don't know.
Barty Bear: He kept laughing during lessons!

What makes more noise than an angry elephant?
Two angry elephants.

Who went into the snake pit and came out alive?
The snake.

What's the difference between a mailbox and a gorilla?
Don't know.
Well I'd never ask you to mail a letter.

FUN AND GAMES

What has four feet, two heads, and runs around screaming? The school tennis doubles team!

Teacher: Tom why are you late for school?
Tom: Well I was dreaming about a football match and it went into extra time.

Ice hockey captain to goalkeeper: Why didn't you stop that puck?
Goalkeeper: I thought that was what the net was for!

What did the referee shout at the alien during a game of football?
Hand-hand-hand-hand-hand-ball!

Hockey player: Coach, I've a great idea on how to win our next match!
Coach: Oh really? Are you leaving then?

It was a freezing cold winter's day, and a man was sitting in his armchair warming himself by the fire. Suddenly, he heard a knock on the door. Reluctantly the man got up and opened the front door. There was nobody to be seen, and the snow drifted in thick and fast. The man was just about to return to the fireside, when he heard a small voice pipe up, "Excuse me, Sir!".
He looked down and saw a little snail shivering on the doorstep.
"Excuse me, Sir, it's so cold out here. Would you let me in so I can warm myself by your fire?"
The grumpy man was annoyed at

being dragged away from his fireside, and said, "Beat it," and kicked the snail out into the middle of the road.

Winter passed, and summer came. This time the grumpy man was sitting watching television, when he heard a knock on the door. He opened the door and, lo and behold, there was the same snail staring up from the doorstep. The snail looked at him accusingly and said, "What did you do that for?"

What goes "7, bonk"?
A spider with a wooden leg.

Teacher: Kim, I'm very disappointed in you for copying Sharon's answers!
Kim: How do you know I copied from her?
Teacher: Because Sharon's written "Don't know," and you've written, "Neither do I"!

Teacher: Jane, did your mother help you with your homework?
Jane: No, I got it wrong all by myself.

Teacher: Sean, name three animals from the ape family.
Sean: Mother Ape, Father Ape, and little Baby Ape.

Jacob: I'm sure my teacher likes me, Dad.
Dad: What makes you think that?
Jacob: Look, she's put kisses next to all my sums.

Teacher: Omar, I asked you to write out this passage six times to improve your terrible handwriting and you've only copied it out five times. Why?
Omar: I can't count either.

Nathan: How were your exam questions?
Carl: Oh, they were easy. It was the answers that were difficult.

John and Nina were having lunch together, when John pulled out his Thermos bottle.
"What's that then?" asked Nina.
"It's my Thermos bottle — it keeps cold things cold, and hot things hot."
"That's brilliant! I'll have to get one of those."
So the next day, Nina comes into work with a new Thermos.
"I see you got one," says John, "what have you got in it today?"
"Oh, just some soup, coffee and ice cream."

DISASTROUS DINNERS

Liam: We always say prayers before we eat our dinner.
Teacher: It's good to see a grateful child.
Liam: Not really, our mother's a terrible cook.

Do you know the difference between jam and manure?
  No.
Well, that's the last time I ask you to make me a jam sandwich!

MEDICAL MISFITS

Patient: Doctor, people keep calling me a liar.
Doctor: I don't believe a word you're saying.

Doctor, doctor I keep thinking I'm a dog.
Well pop up on the couch and we'll discuss it.
I can't. I'm not allowed on the furniture.

Doctor: Is that medicine that I prescribed to improve your memory working?
Patient: What medicine?

Doctor: So, Mr. Brown. How's your wife's lumbago?
Mr. Brown: Not very good.
Doctor: Did you massage the brandy into her back as I instructed?
Mr. Brown: Yes, but then she cricked her neck trying to lick it all off.

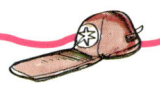

What's the first sign of madness?
Don't know.
Little black hairs in the palms of your hands.

Oh... *(at this point your victim will start looking at their palms).*

And the second sign of madness is looking for them.

Did you hear about the mad scientist who invented non-stick glue?

BEASTLY BONANZA

There was an elephant in my bed last night.
How could you tell?
He had an E embroidered on his nightshirt.

What do you get when a whale sits on you?
Wet.

How can you tell if there's a polar bear in your freezer?
You can't shut the door.

What do you get if you cross a porcupine with a giraffe?
A very long toothbrush.

What's big, brown and hairy and goes up and down?
A bear in an elevator.

Waiter, waiter this water is cloudy...
No, Madam, it's just that your glass is dirty...

Waiter, waiter, this apple pie is revolting!
Well, I'm surprised, the chef here has been making apple pie since before you were born!
Perhaps, but he didn't have to save it for me!

Waiter, waiter, what's this caterpillar doing in my salad?
Look's like he's having lunch, Madam...

A RECIPE FOR DISASTER

Waiter, waiter, it's been at least an hour since I ordered those snails.
Well, Madam, you know how slow snails are…

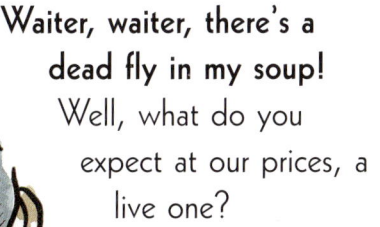

Waiter, waiter, there's a dead fly in my soup!
Well, what do you expect at our prices, a live one?

Waiter, waiter, how can you call this a three course meal?
Well, there's two peas, and a chip, Sir.

Patient: Doctor, I'm terrified of hospitals. You're the first doctor I've ever seen!
Student Doctor: What a coincidence. You're the first patient I've ever seen.

Doctor, doctor, I think I've got double vision.
OK lay down on the couch.
Which one?

Patient: Doctor, I keep thinking I'm invisible.
Doctor: Aagh! A ghost!

Patient: Doctor, people keep being rude to me.
Doctor: Go away you stupid idiot.

Patient: Doctor, I'm so ill.
Doctor: What are your symptoms — do you feel hot?
Patient: Yes.
Doctor: And sweaty?
Patient: Yes.
Doctor: And do you ache?
Patient: Yes, in every bone.
Doctor: Mmmm. Same here. I wonder what we've got?

Hear the one about the mad scientist who crossed a mynah bird with a crocodile?
It bit his arm off and said "Who's a pretty boy then?"

What do you get when you cross a carrier pigeon with a woodpecker?
A bird that knocks before it delivers its message.

A flock of birds were setting off on their annual migration, when the baby bird asked his mother, "Why do we always follow the same leader?"
"Because she's the only one with a map," said his mother.

What's this?
A bird?
Nope.
What then?
Me waving my arms.

Tara: I'd like to have lived in the olden days.
Teacher (interested): Oh really, why?
Tara: Because there wasn't so much history to learn then!

Jimmy: I spoke to a Martian yesterday.
Teacher: But Jimmy, Martians live on Mars!
Jimmy: I know. I really had to shout.

Teacher: Joseph! Your appearance is a disgrace. What would you say if I came into school looking as scruffy as you?
Joseph: I'd be far too polite to mention it, Sir.

Teacher: Now Megan, if I ate ten cakes and then ate another twenty cakes, how many cakes would I have eaten in total?
Megan: Too many.

Teacher: Carlos, how would you spell cough?
Carlos: K-O-F-F.
Teacher: No Carlos, the dictionary spells it **C-O-U-G-H**.
Carlos: But you asked me how I would spell it, not the dictionary, Miss Perez.

HOW DO YOU KEEP AN IDIOT GUESSING?
DON'T KNOW
I'LL TELL YOU NEXT WEEK!

MINDBOGGLERS

Mario: My dad's got a terrible memory.
Luigi: Oh, does he forget everything?
Mario: No, he remembers everything.

Customer: Well, Madame Zara, you claim that you can read minds but I don't believe you!
Madame Zara: I knew you'd say that.

Have I ever told you the memory joke?
  No.
Oops, I've forgotten it.

What's fat and noisy?
A hippo with a pair of cymbals.

Why did the elephant paint the soles of his feet yellow?
So he could hide upside down in a bowl of custard.

Why did the elephant paint his toenails red?
To hide upside down in a bowl of cherries.

But I've never seen an elephant in my custard or in a bowl of cherries!
See it works!

Can a mouse jump higher than a house?
Yes. Houses can't jump.

What do you get when you cross a mouse with a mammoth?
Big holes in the floorboards.

IT'S A SCREAM!

Why did the witch fly on her broomstick to Dracula's castle?

> Because it was too far to walk.

Baby Vampire: Dad, what is a vampire?
Dracula: Be quiet, and drink your shake before it clots.

What's the first thing the monster ate after he had his fang out?
The dentist.

What time is it when a werewolf howls?
Time you were somewhere else.

Why couldn't Frankenstein tango?
Because he had two left feet.

Baby Monster: Dad, I've got a horrible lump on the top of my neck!
Daddy Monster: That's your head.

Doctor: Your face is purple, your tongue is green and your breath is revolting.
Monster: What a relief. I thought there was something wrong with me....

Mrs. Monster: How can I stop myself biting my nails?
Mrs. Vile: Have you tried wearing shoes?

BOING, BONK, AAGH!

What's black and white and goes "boing, boing"?
A nun on a pogo stick.

What's black and white, and goes "boing, boing, ouch!"?
A nun on a pogo stick going under a low bridge.

What's black and white, and black and white, and black and white?
A nun rolling down a hill.

What were Tarzan's last words?
Don't know.
Who greased that vine?